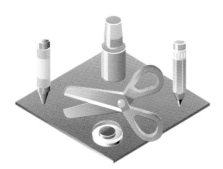

THE
CHILD'S
WORLD

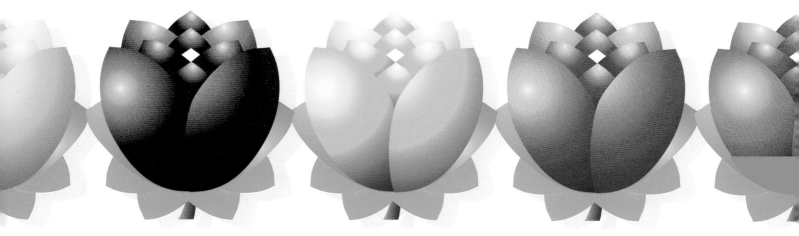

MOTHER'S DAY
CRAFTS

by Jean Eick

Library of Congress Cataloging-in-Publication Data
Eick, Jean. 1947-
Mother's Day Crafts Crafts / by Jean Eick.
p. cm.
Includes index.
Summary: Provides ideas for simple gifts and activities
to celebrate Mother's Day.
ISBN 1-56766-538-1 (library bound : alk. Paper)

1. Holiday decorations — Juvenile literature.
2. Handicraft — Juvenile literature.
[1. Mother's Day. 2. Handicraft.]
I. Title.

TT900.H6E33 1998   98-3249
745.594'1 — dc21   CIP
                                                     AC

GRAPHIC DESIGN & ILLUSTRATION
Robert A. Honey, Seattle

PRODUCTION COORDINATION
James R. Rothaus / James R. Rothaus & Associates

ELECTRONIC PRE-PRESS PRODUCTION
Robert E. Bonaker / Graphic Design & Consulting Company

CONTENTS

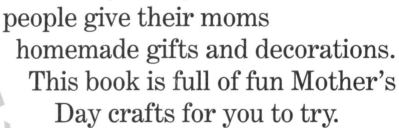

1 Mother's Day is a very special day. It's a time to show how much people care about their mothers. It is also a time to say "Thank you." On Mother's Day, many people give their moms homemade gifts and decorations. This book is full of fun Mother's Day crafts for you to try.

2 Before you start making any craft, be sure to read the directions. Make sure you look at the pictures too, they will help you understand what to do. Go through the list of things you'll need and get everything together. When you're ready, find a good place to work. Now you can begin making your crafts!

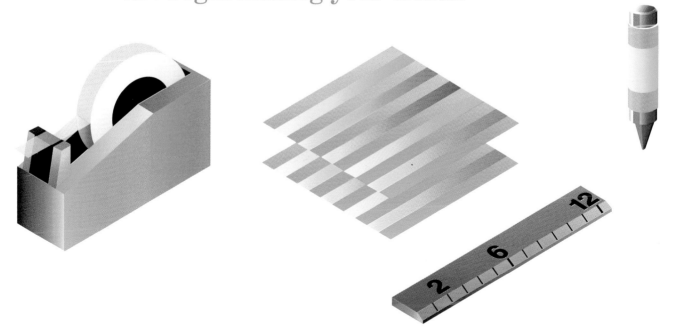

*Moms love flowers.
Instead of real ones,
try making some
of these instead.*

PIPE CLEANER FLOWERS

Things You'll Need

Scissors.

3 Green Pipe Cleaners.

Hole Puncher.

Ruler.

Construction Paper.
1 Pink.
1 White.
1 Green.

Pencil.

Glue.

A Large Drinking Glass.

A Small Drinking Glass.

1 Use the large glass to trace a circle on the pink paper.

2 Carefully cut out the circle.

3 Use the smaller glass to trace a circle on the white paper.

4 Carefully cut out the circle.

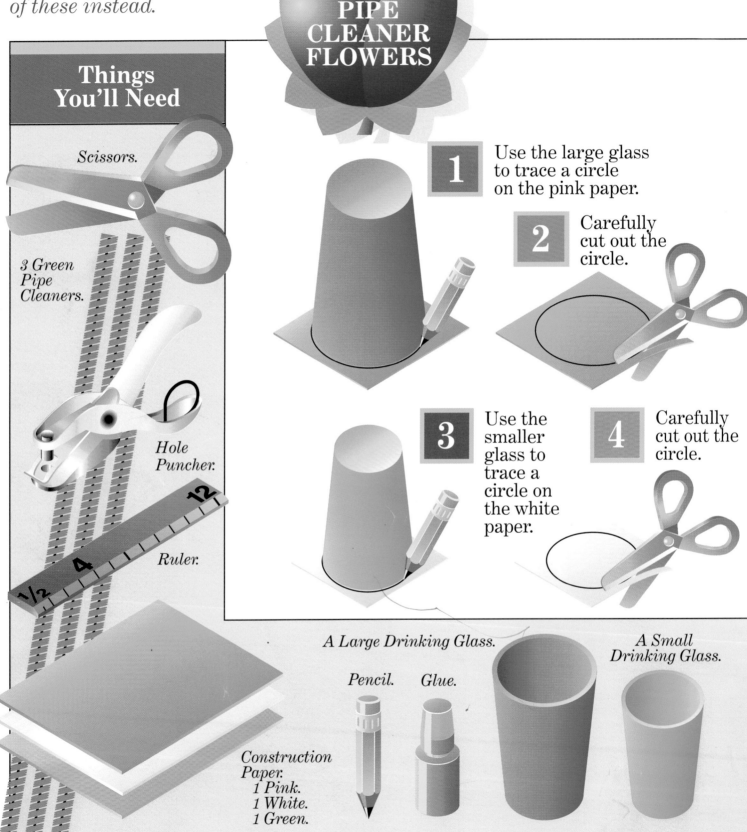

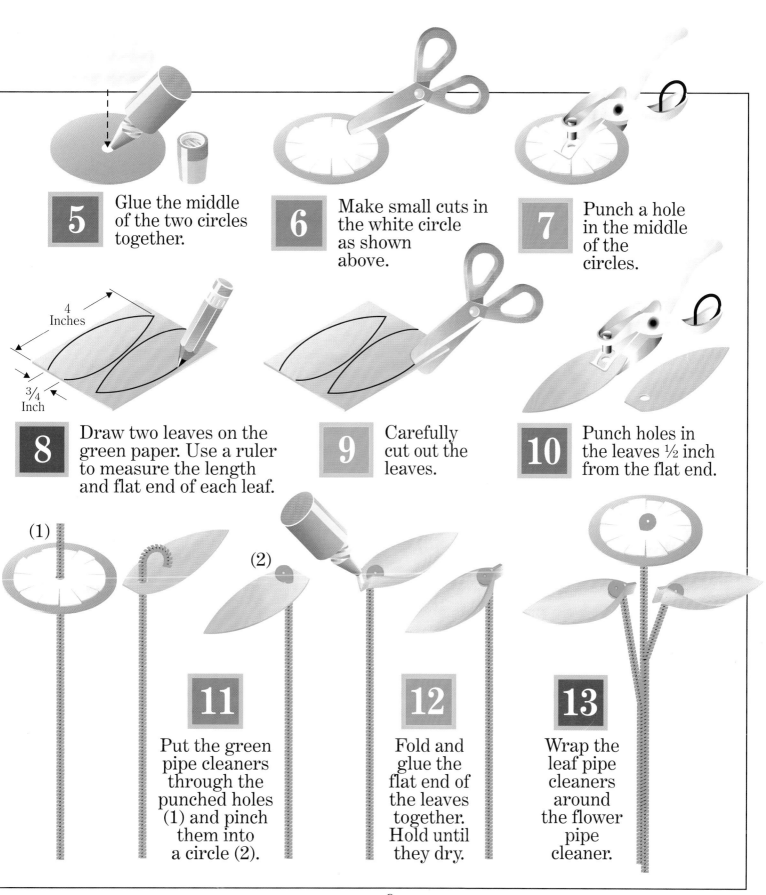

5 Glue the middle of the two circles together.

6 Make small cuts in the white circle as shown above.

7 Punch a hole in the middle of the circles.

4 Inches

3/4 Inch

8 Draw two leaves on the green paper. Use a ruler to measure the length and flat end of each leaf.

9 Carefully cut out the leaves.

10 Punch holes in the leaves ½ inch from the flat end.

(1)

(2)

11 Put the green pipe cleaners through the punched holes (1) and pinch them into a circle (2).

12 Fold and glue the flat end of the leaves together. Hold until they dry.

13 Wrap the leaf pipe cleaners around the flower pipe cleaner.

Here are even
more flowers
you can give
your mom.

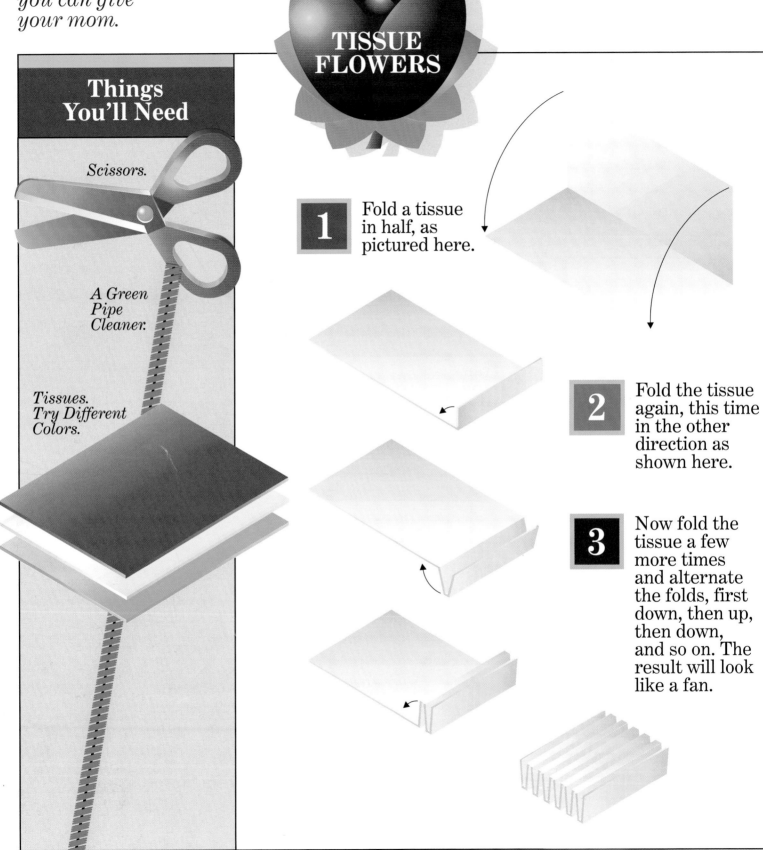

TISSUE FLOWERS

Things You'll Need

Scissors.

A Green Pipe Cleaner.

Tissues. Try Different Colors.

1 Fold a tissue in half, as pictured here.

2 Fold the tissue again, this time in the other direction as shown here.

3 Now fold the tissue a few more times and alternate the folds, first down, then up, then down, and so on. The result will look like a fan.

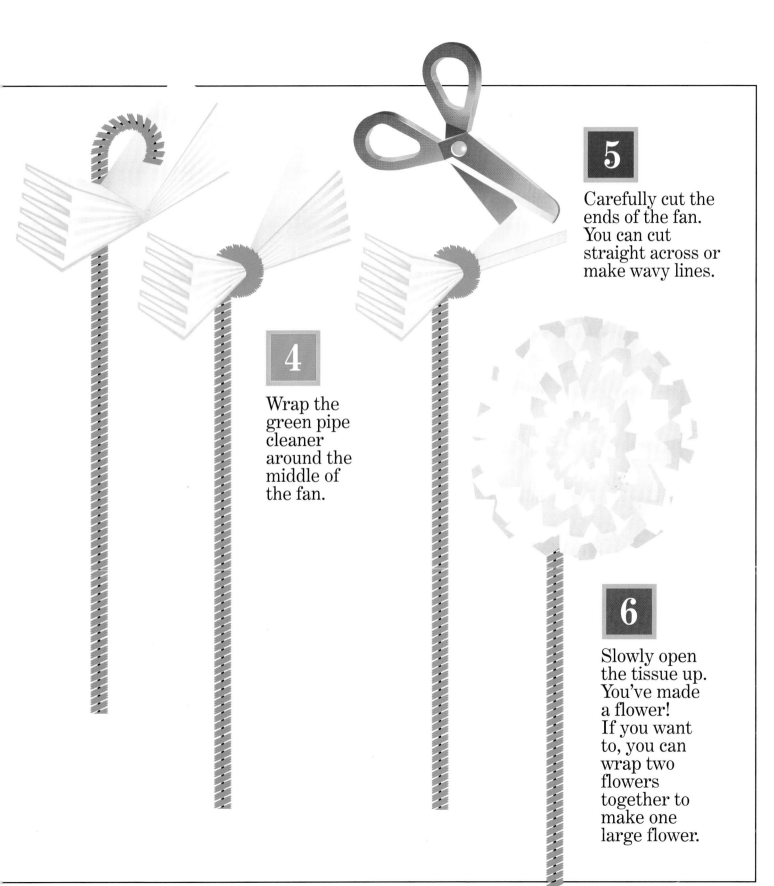

5

Carefully cut the ends of the fan. You can cut straight across or make wavy lines.

4

Wrap the green pipe cleaner around the middle of the fan.

6

Slowly open the tissue up. You've made a flower! If you want to, you can wrap two flowers together to make one large flower.

11

Your mom can use these pretty pots for planting or to put candles inside.

PAINTED POTS

Things You'll Need

A Clay Pot. *Any size works, but small ones are best.*

Acrylic *(uh-krih-lik)* **Paints.** *Ask an adult where you can get some.*

Pencil.   *A Paint Brush.*

A Cup Of Water For Cleaning The Brush.

1 Make sure the outside of the pot is clean. Wipe off any dirt or dust you can see.

2 Think about what you want to paint, then lightly draw it on the pot.

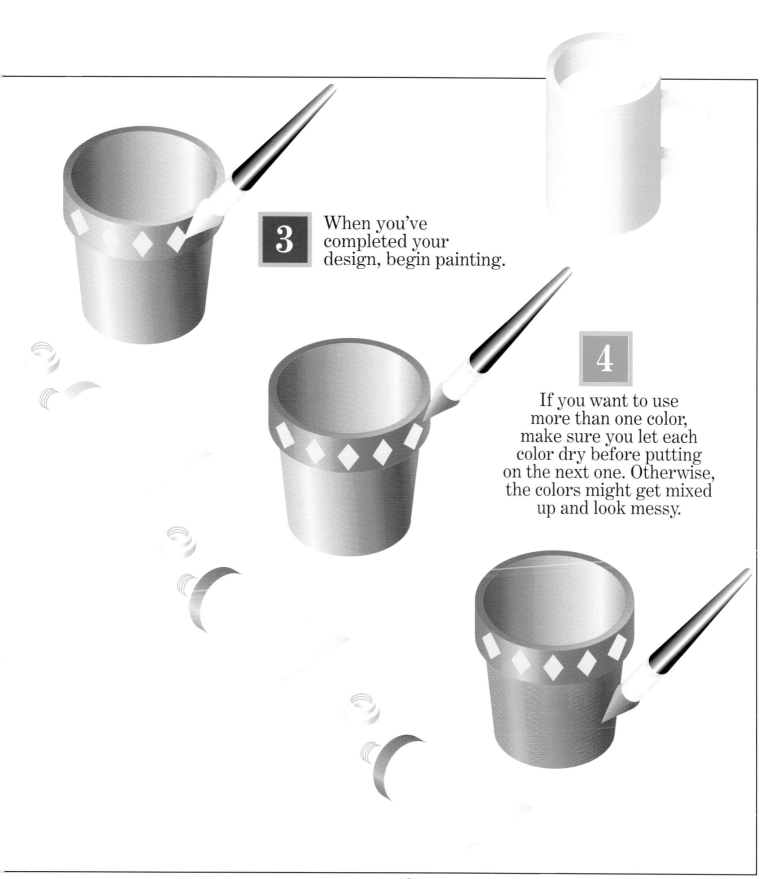

3 When you've completed your design, begin painting.

4 If you want to use more than one color, make sure you let each color dry before putting on the next one. Otherwise, the colors might get mixed up and look messy.

Moms often like to send quick notes to their friends. Make your mom some special note cards she will love.

DECORATED CARDS

Things You'll Need

6 Pieces Of Plain Paper.

Things for Decorating

Crayons, or Paints. *Glue.* *Colored Markers.*

Glitter. *Buttons and Stickers.*

Ribbon.

1 Fold each piece of paper in half. Now you can make six different cards.

2 Decorate the front of each card only. Start by making a "Thank You" card.

3 Make another one that says "Hello."

4 Make one that says "Happy Birthday."

5 Write one that says "To My Friend."

6 Write another one that says "Just A Note."

7 Leave the sixth card empty.

8 Make envelopes for your cards by following the directions on pages 21. Wrap all the cards and envelopes together in a neat bunch and tie with a ribbon.

This looks great almost anywhere— especially on Mom's desk or in her kitchen.

FLOWER VASE
OR
PENCIL HOLDER

Pencil Holders.

Things You'll Need

Scissors.

A Short Container for a Pencil Holder.

MILK

A Tall Container for a Flower Vase.

Glue.

SALAD DRESSING

Wrapping Paper.

1

First, wash and dry the container you are going to use. If you use a small milk carton for the pencil holder, carefully cut off the top.

MILK

2

Cut some wrapping paper and roll it around the outside of the container. Glue the wrapping paper in place and carefully trim off any excess paper.

Things for Decorating

Ribbon.

Glitter.

Buttons.

Stickers

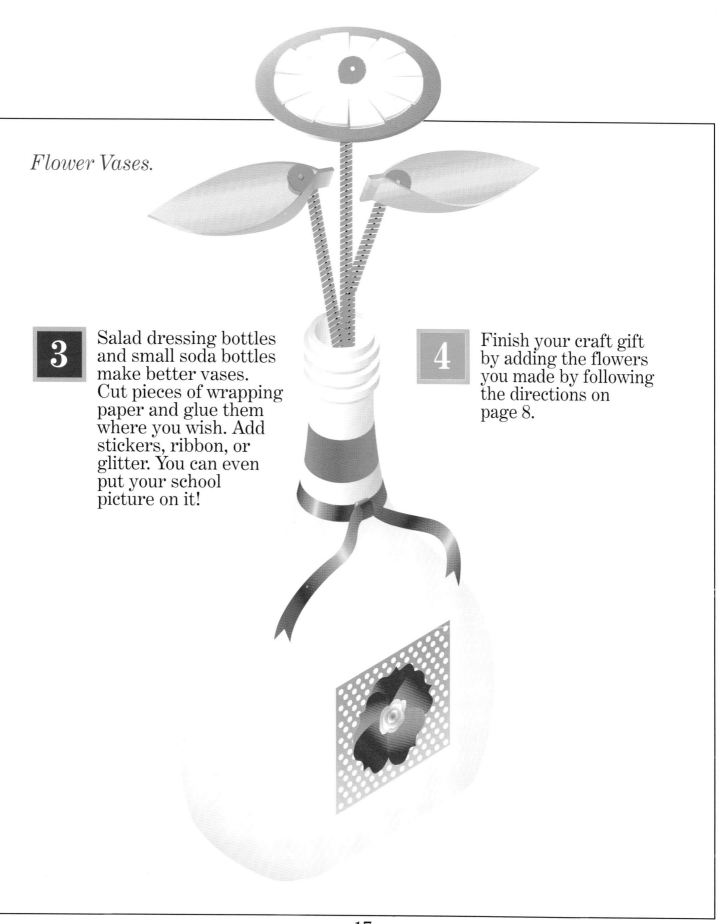

Flower Vases.

3 Salad dressing bottles and small soda bottles make better vases. Cut pieces of wrapping paper and glue them where you wish. Add stickers, ribbon, or glitter. You can even put your school picture on it!

4 Finish your craft gift by adding the flowers you made by following the directions on page 8.

Mother's Day is a great time to give your mom a special card. Write a nice message inside thanking your mom.

CARDS

1 Fold the paper to the size you want your card to be. Folding it once will make a large card.

2 Folding it twice will make a small card.

3 Decorate the front of the card.

4 Write a message on the inside of the card. You can decorate the inside, too. Don't forget to sign your name.

Things for Decorating

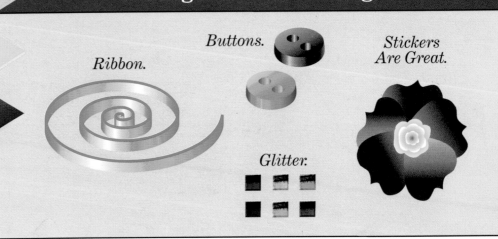

Ribbon.

Buttons.

Stickers Are Great.

Glitter.

You can make Mother's Day cards different ways.
Here are some ideas for making your cards even more special:

1

Place your hand print on the front of a large card. Just dip your hand in some water soluble paint and then press it onto the paper. Wash right away.

2

Glue colored paper strips and a white cotton ball to the front of the card to make a flower.

3

Cut construction paper strips and glue them into rings. Then glue the rings to the front of the card.

4

Glue a picture of yourself and your mom on the card. Decorate all around it with whatever you want.

You can even make your own envelopes to fit your cards!

ENVELOPES

Things You'll Need

Scissors.

Construction Paper, Wrapping Paper, or Paper Bag.

Pencil.

Tape or Glue.

Ruler.

To make a square envelope:

1 Cut out the front of a plain paper bag. It will take an 8 inch square piece of paper to hold a 5¼ inch square card.

2 Cut out a square 8 inches high and 8 inches across. Measure and put an "X" in the center of the square.

3 Fold three of the corners so they cover the "X". Tape or glue the corners so they'll stay in place.

4 Place your card inside, then fold the top down and tape it shut.

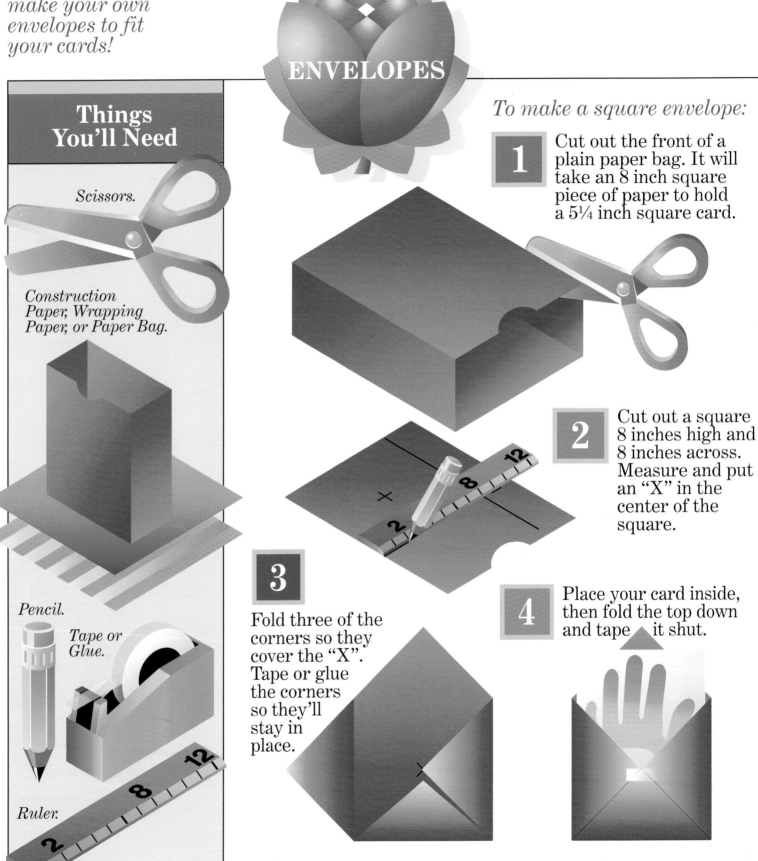

To make an envelope that isn't square:

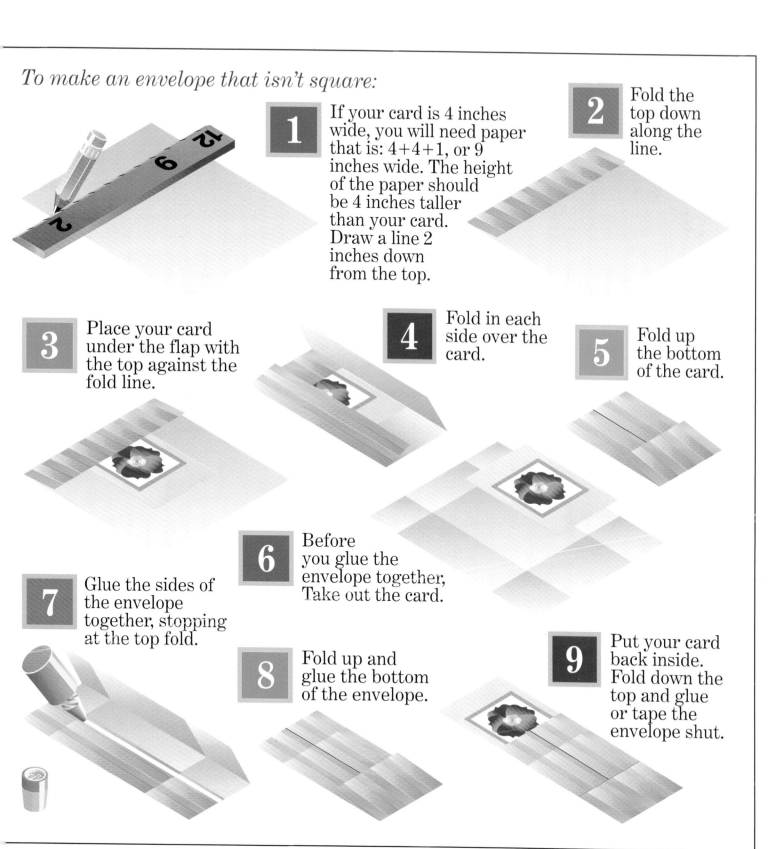

1 If your card is 4 inches wide, you will need paper that is: 4+4+1, or 9 inches wide. The height of the paper should be 4 inches taller than your card. Draw a line 2 inches down from the top.

2 Fold the top down along the line.

3 Place your card under the flap with the top against the fold line.

4 Fold in each side over the card.

5 Fold up the bottom of the card.

6 Before you glue the envelope together, Take out the card.

7 Glue the sides of the envelope together, stopping at the top fold.

8 Fold up and glue the bottom of the envelope.

9 Put your card back inside. Fold down the top and glue or tape the envelope shut.

Here are some fun things to do to celebrate Mother's Day. Try them all. Show your mom how special she is.

ACTIVITIES

1 Write notes saying "Thank you" to your mom for some of the things she does for you. They can be things such as:

Thanks, Mom, for reading to me.
Thanks, Mom, for washing my clothes.
Thanks, Mom, for baking my favorite cookies.

2 Set the table before anyone else does. Tie all the napkins with pretty ribbons. You can even put decorations you made from this book in the middle of the table!

3 Tie a pretty ribbon around your mom's favorite candy bar. Put it on her pillow for a bedtime surprise. Leave it with a card that tells her how special she is.

4 Start an outdoor garden with your mom. With her help, plant some seeds inside a pot or small container. Water the seeds and give them plenty of sunlight. When they're ready, take the pot outside and help your mom plant them in her garden or flowerbed.

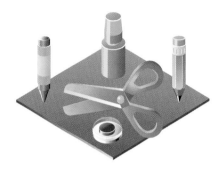

13/03

MG